LEADERSHIP AT WORK

THE POWER OF SERVANT LEADERSHIP

(Leadership Advancement Series Book One)

JOHN MAXIMILIAN

Leadership at Work: The Power of Servant Leadership by John Maximilian (Leadership Advancement Series Book One)

Published by John Maximilian

Copyright © 2022 John Maximilian All rights reserved.

No portion of this book may be reproduced in any form without permission from the publisher, except in the case of brief quotations embodied in reviews and certain other non-commercial uses permitted by U.S. copyright law.

Table of Content

DEDICATION 7

INTRODUCTION 9

CHAPTER 1..13

   REDEFINING LEADERSHIP IN THE WORKPLACE 13
      The Value of Leadership in the Workplace 14

CHAPTER 2..17

   THE ATTRIBUTES OF AN EFFECTIVE LEADER IN THE WORKPLACE 17
      1. Communication...17
      2. Compassion/Empathy..17
      3. Approachability..18
      4. Kindness 18
      5. Passion 19
      6. Firmness...19
      5 Inspiring Traits of a Great Leader in the Workplace 19
      1. Confidence 19
      2. Empathy...20
      3. Vision 21
      4. Honesty..21
      5. Decisiveness 22

CHAPTER 3..25

   LEADERSHIP STYLES IN THE WORKPLACE 25

CHAPTER 4..29

   HOW TO STRENGTHEN YOUR LEADERSHIP ABILITIES AT WORK 29
      1. Recognize Your Strengths and Weaknesses...........................29
      2. Enhance Interpersonal Communication 30
      3. Set Realistic Goals..30
      4. Be Inclusive 31

CHAPTER 5..33

      What Characterizes a Successful Leader in the Workplace?......................38

1. Leaders Create a Vision ... 38
2. Leaders Work Well With a Team ... 40
3. Leaders Enable Success ... 42
4. Leaders Are Flexible ... 43
The Good Leader and His Team Colors ... 45
Gold ... 47
Blue ... 47
Green ... 48
Orange ... 48

CHAPTER 6 ... 51

THREE THINGS LEADERS DON'T DO ... 51
1. Management Vs. Leadership ... 51
2. Personality or Trait Theory ... 53
3. Hierarchy ... 54
Leadership and Team Management ... 55

CHAPTER 7 ... 63

HOW TO BECOME A BETTER LEADER IN THE WORKPLACE ... 63
Rules for Effective Leadership ... 65
1. Seek To Motivate Others ... 66
2. Show High Emotional Intelligence ... 67
3. Demonstrate Hard Work ... 69
4. Pay Attention To Your Workers ... 70
5. Good Leaders Avoid Micromanagement ... 71

CHAPTER 8 ... 73

THE POWER OF SERVANT LEADERSHIP ... 73
What exactly is Servant Leadership? ... 74
Relationship Qualities and Abilities For Good Servant Leadership ... 77
1. Availability ... 78
2. Approachability ... 78
3. Promoting Peaceful Relationships ... 78
4. Proper Usage Of Power ... 78
5. Self-Motivated ... 79
6. Provide Support ... 79
7. Fostering Team Spirit and Motivation ... 80

- 8. Confidentiality 80
- 9. Clear Communication 80
- 10. Group Dynamics Understanding 80

Destructive Traits A Leader Should Avoid 81
- 1. Dismissive. 81
- 2. Egotistical. 81
- 3. Lacking Empathy. 82
- 4. Grudge-bearing. 82
- 5. Pessimism. 82
- 6. Inconsistency. 82
- 7. Lack Of Transparency. 83
- 8. Exhausted. 83

CHAPTER 9 85

CHARACTERISTICS OF THE SERVANT-LEADER 85

CHAPTER 10 89

THE ADVANTAGES OF SERVANT LEADERSHIP 89

Drawbacks of Servant Leadership 91
- 1. Modesty. 94
- 2. Adhere to Your Happiness. 95
- 3. Think Big. 96
- 4. SWOT On Yourself. 97
- 5. Vision. 98
- 6. Perseverance. 98
- 7. Find a Mentor. 98
- 8. Be Authentic. 99
- 9. Keep Your Word. 100
- 10. Give Generously. 100

CHAPTER 11 103

CONCLUSION 103

DEDICATION

I would like to dedicate this book to the following people:

My family: You are the reason why I wrote this book, dad your sacrifices allowed me to live the life of my dreams.

Introduction

What would happen if you completely turned upside down the traditional hierarchy and leadership model of an organization? You'd think there'd be chaos, but this wouldn't be the case.

Servant leadership is a style of leadership that employs this approach.

According to the principles of servant leadership, focus on empowering and elevating others rather than on advancing one's own interests is essential for everyone's success.

Fundamentally, this style of leadership aims to create a workplace where individual goals and objectives don't interfere with the group's mission.

So whether you're a manager, CEO, or business owner, becoming a successful servant leader is crucial to your professional development. What, then, characterizes a servant leader, and how do you develop into one?

There is no one recipe for becoming a successful servant leader; they come in a variety of sizes and shapes. In this book, we'll talk about some key traits that will help you develop into a successful servant leader at work, describe some common leadership styles, and provide some straightforward but useful advice you can use to hone your leadership abilities right away.

Being a servant leader entails being accountable to the people you oversee. However, do you know how to organize your time, make plans, and inspire those around you? How can you develop into a manager or colleague that everyone enjoys working with?

This book answers this question, as well as many others. You will gain more knowledge about this style of leadership and how to apply it to improve your organization.

Every organization needs effective leadership. Organizations with strong leadership are typically more productive, competitive, and adaptable to change. Learn how you can get more commitment and motivation from those you lead, even if it's your family, by developing a clearer vision of where you're going and why.

Since there is no such thing as a perfect leader and because change is a constant, it is crucial that you continue honing your leadership abilities and keeping up with developments in your chosen field. This book will lead you and assist you in determining the aspects of servant leadership on which you should focus and excel. Because only one in a million people may be born with leadership qualities, a large percentage of effective leaders are taught. It's possible for you to learn, and I'll demonstrate how to do it in detail for you. I'll guide you through each process step-by-step until you have mastered everything required to succeed as a strong servant leader.

CHAPTER 1

Redefining Leadership in the Workplace

Effective leadership in the workplace entails maximizing the potential of those around you and uniting individuals with different backgrounds, perspectives, and styles in service of a common objective.

This calls for the capability of positively influencing other team members through traits like charisma, confidence, and vision, or even just by demonstrating how to get things done. A leader doesn't hesitate to take the initiative and exhibit the behavior and dedication that they anticipate from their team.

Despite being two distinct ideas, management and leadership are frequently used synonymously. Leaders in the workplace set the example, lead by example, and coordinate efforts to achieve success while managers keep things organized by supervising and energizing to ensure effective performance.

To harmonize the company's values and objectives with those of its employees, every successful organization needs leaders within its ranks. Additionally, while effective leadership skills can be taught and acquired over the course of a career, some innate traits are advantageous.

Being a good leader is not something that everyone is naturally good at.

The Value of Leadership in the Workplace

Having capable and forward-thinking leaders can help a business in many ways, including the following:

• Company morale: Leaders who can successfully foster a sense of trust among their team members, keep them informed, and convey a vision for the future, foster a productive workplace that people can identify with.

• Employee Engagement: This is largely influenced by the quality of interpersonal connections and the leadership style. Gallup estimates that team leaders alone are responsible for 70% of the variation in team engagement. Employees seek meaning and purpose in their work, and they view their leader as the one who can give them both.

- Reduced turnover: Increasing employee engagement is crucial for higher retention rates. The ability to keep your best and brightest employees increases productivity and morale while also saving money in today's fiercely competitive labor market.

- Adaptability: Effective leaders can unite everyone to work toward a common objective. This is especially helpful during transitional periods when overcoming challenges requires a cohesive team effort built on respect for one another and a clear goal.

CHAPTER 2

The Attributes Of an Effective Leader In The Workplace

1. Communication

An effective leader at work is one who sets clear expectations and is a strong communicator. Additionally, they encourage open communication among the members of their team. When it comes to using chats, emails, and messaging groups to unite their team around work-related concerns, a great leader goes above and beyond. They provide more than simply networking resources; they also aid in the growth of good communication skills.

2. Compassion/Empathy

A good boss shows their staff that they care about them. They demonstrate their concern for their employees and their perception of them as more than just human chattel by recalling the specifics of their lives and asking follow-up inquiries (in a non-intrusive manner) about wives, kids, parents, and life events.

3. Approachability

A good leader is someone who followers feel comfortable approaching with queries or grievances. The office door must occasionally be shut. At other times, it should be left open and perhaps provide some sweets or coffee for any straggling staff. They should know your office is a safe haven they can go to for aid rather than dread it like they did the principal's.

4. Kindness

Whether it's renting a food cart for lunch or taking the whole company to the movies, everyone appreciates a leader who goes above and beyond for the team. Bosses and managers will find that they have a far more productive staff on their payroll if they utilize prizes to inspire their team rather than threats and punishments.

5. Passion

You'll discover that setting an excellent example as the team leader is the finest course of action. Your employees will catch your passion if you are invested in the goals of your firm and care about what it accomplishes. To stay on the cutting edge in your field, read up frequently, network at events, and go to conferences.

6. Firmness

Nobody wants a boss who is a dictator, but they also don't want someone who is weak. If necessary, a smart leader will know when to politely put their foot down and break up water-cooler parties or have a conversation with an employee about poorly managed time.

5 Inspiring Traits of a Great Leader in the Workplace

1. Confidence

Few people will choose to emulate someone who is obviously not confident in themselves.

When a leader lacks confidence, it suggests that either they don't know what they're doing or that they are the incorrect candidate for the position. Uncertainty at the top quickly permeates a company and can have a demoralizing impact that is challenging to reverse.

While confidence can be fostered in a supportive and encouraging environment, some people are naturally more confident than others.

2. Empathy

Empathy is the ability to comprehend the circumstances of those around you.

This is essential for good workplace leadership because it facilitates effective communication and builds trust among team members. People who lack empathy and an awareness of how their actions affect others make it difficult to develop lasting relationships.

Empathetic leaders understand how to interact with people in trying circumstances and can modify their style to suit the unique needs and personality of each person.

3. Vision

Workplace leaders differ from managers in that they have a clear vision, and how to get there.

So, in order to be visionary, a leader must have a thorough understanding of their organization, its current environment, its strengths and weaknesses, and the ability to see beyond current obstacles. Additionally, they must be able to explain their vision to other team members.

4. Honesty

Leadership integrity entails adhering to a set of values despite any difficulties. People look to their leaders as a moral compass and a reliable source of direction during trying times.

This entails having the humility to acknowledge mistakes when they happen and making a point of taking something away from them. It entails being receptive to the thoughts and opinions of others, particularly those who might be better qualified in a particular field. It also entails having the guts to provide candid feedback, even if it can make for a tense meeting.

Even though it isn't always simple to be honest in trying circumstances, doing so is crucial for gaining respect over time. Honesty also aids in preventing unneeded issues or misunderstandings brought on by broken promises or erroneous expectations.

5. Decisiveness

Leadership decisions determine whether a company succeeds or fails. They must have confidence in their ability to make resolute, assertive decisions and uphold them.

Leaders who are indecisive run the risk of losing the trust of their team because they come across as unmotivated and unwilling to accept responsibility. Effective leadership calls for quick decision-making, supported by in-depth understanding of the circumstances and the willingness to accept advice from others.

Making decisions requires taking responsibility for both good and bad choices. It entails bearing responsibility when something goes wrong and sharing success with the entire team when something goes well.

CHAPTER 3

Leadership Styles in the Workplace

Effective leadership in the workplace comes in a variety of styles and forms; there is no one approach that works for everyone. You might take the lead in various ways, depending on the circumstance:

- Collaboration: Leaders who work well with others prioritize delegating tasks to them. They prefer to operate in a democratic manner, combining their knowledge and using all of the tools at their disposal to reach decisions. When quick decisions are required, this leadership style can be problematic but is very beneficial for teams with strong bonds and a sense of community.

- Charismatic: With their engaging personalities and social skills, charismatic leaders enthuse and inspire their teams. They enhance a company's morale and reputation by fostering a positive work environment through their close relationships and empathic nature, as well as through their dedication and enthusiasm for their jobs. This type of leadership is useful for giving people a boost of energy during a trying time, but a personality-driven leader may find it difficult to make difficult decisions that might upset others.

- Servant: Servant leaders put their employees' needs first, providing the best conditions for them to flourish and reach their full potential as workers. This style of leadership places a strong emphasis on social and empathetic abilities, adopts a nurturing rather than coercive approach, and has faith that, given the right conditions, teams will produce effective outcomes on their own. In a quick-paced, cutthroat business with high standards and ambitious goals, it might not be the best option.

- Coaching: Coaching leaders use a one-on-one approach to their team, encouraging and educating each member to perform at their highest level. This coaching approach is perfect for managers who enjoy imparting knowledge to their teams, fostering growth and development, and assisting team members in becoming authorities in their respective fields. This strategy, though, may not be suitable for everyone as it can make staff members feel overworked and overanalyzed; some people would rather make their own mistakes and learn from them.

CHAPTER 4

How to Strengthen Your Leadership Abilities at Work

Learning and improving leadership skills in the workplace is a continuous process; to become a better leader, practice the following skills on a regular basis.

1. Recognize Your Strengths and Weaknesses

You might have a natural aptitude for leadership and already exhibit many of the necessary traits. Building self-awareness of your strengths and weaknesses is still essential. Regular team feedback is a great way to accomplish this, and a technique known as 360-degree feedback has proven to be particularly beneficial and efficient.

This type of anonymous communication, delivered from the viewpoints of various team members, provides a special insight into how others view your leadership abilities. Without the conflict that could arise in franker and more direct discussions, you'll discover precisely which areas you might need to improve.

2. Enhance Interpersonal Communication

You must engage in active listening exercises with your team because communication is a two-way street. Pay attention to what people are saying, interpret their body language, and spot potential issues before they undermine team morale.

You must always be approachable as a leader and show genuine interest in other people's perspectives. Maintain open lines of communication by scheduling regular one-on-one meetings, and always follow through on your commitments to assist. Genuine leadership demands that flattering words be matched by effective deeds.

3. Set Realistic Goals

To maintain focus and consistency, set both long-term and short-term objectives. Keep your objectives challenging but doable; otherwise, team members may become demoralized by seemingly impossible goals that ultimately fail.

Goals can be set during gatherings like your end-of-year review and changed as necessary throughout the year. Don't forget to acknowledge successes, offer advice that is focused on finding solutions, and leave your team members with a clear understanding of how to move forward.

4. Be Inclusive

Not everything needs to be done by the leader in order for them to be effective. Ask for help and advice from others, and when it makes sense, trust your team by giving them important tasks to complete. Giving employees responsibility fosters their sense of ownership in the business as a whole and fosters a stimulating and inspiring work environment.

By taking the time to support specific team members when they're struggling or under pressure, you can also help your team members develop empathy for one another. Recognize when someone might require help before they have to ask for it, and set an example for others to follow. Leaders who don't mind getting their hands dirty and aiding in routine tasks can motivate and inspire those around them.

CHAPTER 5
Leadership And Teamwork

A strong and positive teamwork is defined by a leader who has a vision and the ability to inspire his or her team to work toward the realization of that vision.

The team's competence and diversity pose no threat to the leader in the slightest. Instead, a strong team leader encourages team members to constantly strive for quality improvement by having a conversation with them about what constitutes quality, what is required to perform and finish the job, and what it looks like.

Let's dissect all of that into its constituent elements. The first is a leader's role is clearly defined. Every team, in my opinion, needs a leader. Someone must be in charge and responsible for making the final choices.

Team members are allowed to alternate as the team's leader as long as everyone is aware of who is in charge at all times. Making some individuals the project leaders for tasks that fall within their competence is another variant on that concept. However, there must always be no doubt among co-workers as to who is in charge of the project or day.

A vision is necessary for the leader. Beginning with the end in mind, Covey's second habit, is comparable to this. A real leader builds the final product twice: once in the mind and once in the final form. Leading people toward a hazy vision is impossible. Simply put, people lack the motivation to pursue what is not certain.

Having the vision alone won't motivate co-workers to work toward the same objective. A strong team leader is able to show each team member how the final product or service will benefit them and what their specific contribution is to achieving that goal..

How does the cleaner enhance the experience of the spectators at a professional football game?

By offering a spotless, orderly restroom environment. The cleaner is more likely to fulfil his duties enthusiastically if he views himself as an important part of the team in the overall objective and receives good praise for it.

Having a clearly defined mission that everyone, ideally, has contributed to defining is another element of being able to motivate one's teammates. If not, team members can at least agree to the already created team mission.

This becomes crucial when team members are at odds with one another. It is helpful to have a pre-established method to gauge the resolution when there is a dispute to be resolved. Every solution is evaluated in relation to the mission and its potential to advance the team toward or away from the end objective.

Another benefit of having a mission that has been approved by the entire team is that it can improve teamwork. Individual egos are among the hardest things to control on a team. Small-scale jealousies and a competitive attitude may exist, which may prevent the best team from working together. A strategy to reduce this risk of failure is the mission statement.

The mission continues to be the focal point against which everything else is measured. A person's actions can help or damage the mission, and they should be handled accordingly. The group's objective must always come before any individual's wants or ego. Backstabbing and jealousy have no place on a team.

The knowledge and diversity of his or her staff pose no threat to a strong leader. The most effective leaders are constantly looking for information from the workers on the front lines. The leader's hands are bound behind his or her back without input from the squad.

Leveraging team members' areas of expertise is also essential. Leaders are unable to be experts in all fields. There will be team members whose talents and skills are superior to the leader in some respects. A wise leader will request assistance when necessary.

Additionally, this is a time to value variety and individuality. It actually has no utility to have a team of individuals that all perform the same tasks in essentially the same manner. It would be easier for one individual to do the task than to assemble a diverse team.

The heterogeneity of a team is what gives it value. The team's creativity and ingenuity will be ignited by listening to opinions and suggestions from those who think and act in novel ways. This is the essence of masterminding. Profit from the wealth already present.

Finally, a good leader sets a high standard. He or she does not demand mediocrity or apathy from his team. It is simple to replace what is average or substandard. When a leader expects his or her team to perform to the best of their abilities, the team is then tasked with continuously improving. The task is never completed. The team should always be reviewing the initiatives taken, and members should feel free to suggest improvements.

A good leader empowers his or her teammates, as I previously stated. This is achieved through creating an atmosphere that meets needs. The team members must get along and trust that the leader and the business are looking out for their interests. They need to be valued, heard, and appreciated. Within the confines of their duties, individuals must be allowed to make decisions, and they must enjoy what they are doing.

Additionally, it is essential that team members feel comfortable. This demonstrates that they have no fear at all. The empowerment of the entire team depends on the team leader creating this climate.

What Characterizes a Successful Leader in the Workplace?

1. Leaders Create a Vision

A vision is a depiction of your ideal future self that is plausible, compelling, and appealing. Vision offers guidance, clarifies priorities, and provides benchmarks for success.

Leaders understand the realities of the present while keeping their vision in mind. They then work to make that vision a reality by incorporating it into everything they do and by establishing links between it and employee productivity.

Leaders take into account how their industry is likely to change and how their rivals are likely to act. They consider how they can successfully innovate and reshape their companies and strategies to compete in upcoming markets. Additionally, they validate their ideas with key stakeholders and by identifying key risks with tools like scenario analysis.

As a result, leaders take the initiative to solve issues, plan for the future, and refuse to accept the status quo.

People must be able to see, feel, comprehend, and embrace a vision for it to be compelling.

Inspirational leaders paint a vivid picture of the world as it will be when their goals are achieved. They share motivating tales and make their visions understandable through relatable examples.

This is an example of how leadership combines the analytical side of vision creation with the passion for shared values to create something that has meaning for the people they lead.

2. Leaders Work Well With a Team

Without contributions from others, leaders cannot realize their vision. A leader's capacity for inspiring others and fostering teamwork is what enables them to carry out their vision. As a result, having good people skills is essential for effective leadership.

Leaders must have a thorough understanding of, respect for, and ability to bring out the best in each member of their team. Understanding team dynamics will be beneficial in this situation.

Effective leaders are aware of and take into account the needs and opinions of all levels of their followers. The ability to take proactive, appropriate action to support engagement and retention rests with leaders who pay close attention to how people feel about their work and what personally motivates them.

People are motivated primarily by how much they feel valued. Effective team leaders find ways to show their appreciation for the accomplishments of their teammates.

Another fundamental leadership quality is the capacity to delegate tasks to others and empower them. If done well, it can give leaders more time to concentrate on larger-scale strategy, bring new perspectives to the vision, and inspire the team. However, this depends on a culture of trust and confidence within the workplace.

Additionally, effective leaders search for potential leaders in others. You can create a setting where you can guarantee long-term success by encouraging the development of leadership skills within your team. Self-sabotage occurs when a leader keeps his or her followers in check out of concern for maintaining control.

3. Leaders Enable Success

At the start of a new project, enthusiasm can be particularly high. But it's up to the leaders to direct their team toward the goal and give them the resources they need to get there.

People require objectives and benchmarks that are closely related to the vision.

Reiterating the vision in terms of its impact and seizing numerous opportunities to communicate it and its pertinent objectives in an enticing and engaging manner can help things become more ingrained.

Leaders must make sure that the work necessary to deliver results is managed effectively, either by themselves or by assigning it to a specific manager or team of managers.

They'll also provide team members with the knowledge and skills they need to carry out their duties and realize the vision. In order to achieve this, they regularly provide and receive feedback, train and coach employees, and promote cooperation and skill sharing throughout the entire organization.

Another crucial skill for leaders is change management because introducing and implementing the vision will probably call for many people to adopt new behaviors, procedures, and roles as well as give them some time to adjust.

4. Leaders Are Flexible

Leaders must be flexible, understanding when to shift their focus and embracing change.

For instance, the shift toward virtual and hybrid environments as well as the globalization of business are two of the most important influences on how leadership is practiced in organizations today.

Marshall Goldsmith, an author and executive coach, identified five emerging traits that he thought would become more crucial for future leaders back in 2003. They still hold true today. They are the ability to:

- Think globally.
- Appreciate cultural diversity.
- Develop technological know-how.
- Forge partnerships and alliances.
- Share leadership.

Depending on the situation, leaders can apply various leadership philosophies. For instance, a direct style is frequently the best when working with new hires or in situations where quick decisions are necessary; on the other hand, an experienced team benefits from a more hands-off approach. Similar to this, some circumstances call for greater attention to the task at hand while others call for greater focus on developing relationships.

More and more, workers are choosing to work for leaders who provide the best learning opportunities, challenges, and a culture that makes staying worthwhile beyond the bare minimum of financial security.

In this situation, a less authoritarian and more consultative style of leadership is probably more effective; transformational leadership is a particularly helpful model.

The Good Leader and His Team Colors

Being a leader may be quite difficult. As leaders we don't always get the luxury to choose who is on our team. Most of the time, a leader inherits a team, of which most of the members have been working there many years and longer than the leader, and may even know more about the work than the leader. That notwithstanding, one of the responsibilities of a leader is to motivate the team to all work together towards the common goal. This can really be a strong challenge. All too often the team is usually comprised of very diverse members, and these members know their own strengths, weaknesses, and work styles. The team's effectiveness is also often complicated by internal squabbles and personal conflicts. Along with managing this team, the leader also has to deliver the outcomes demanded by their superiors.

Understanding the different personality traits of team members can be quite helpful for leaders. The leader may exploit each team member's unique abilities for the benefit of the group by being aware of the different personality types and by giving them assignments where they naturally shine. A leader can develop good communication skills by considering the requirements, values, and preferred methods of work of various team members.

Working with and leveraging the personalities on the team's abilities and working styles can help a competent leader get the best results. The leader can achieve a fruitful balance and harmony within the team by appropriately utilizing each member's abilities and making up for any inadequacies.

A brief summary of the different values and working styles of the four main personality types illustrates the importance of this knowledge being part of the successful leadership working toolbox. The colors Orange, Blue, Gold, and Green, will be used to describe the four different personality types.

Gold

The Gold employee takes work and responsibility very seriously. Gold-level personalities strive to succeed and be successful members of the team. Recognition, incentives, and awards are favorably received by them. However, Gold team members require well defined roles and structures, specific deadlines, and confirmation from higher-ups that they are on the correct road.

Blue

The Blue personality needs an open, social atmosphere to be able work well. They place a high value on relationships and require the freedom to foster such ties with clients, employers, and co-workers. Strong Blues find conflict and fierce rivalry painful, but they thrive in environments where they can be upbeat, creative, and service-oriented.

Green

A Green personality is more noted for expertise rather than people skills. They are great at working on projects involving facts, data, research, and analysis. Greens excel at designing, comprehending, and developing strategies for complicated systems. The Green place a high value on facts, but they struggle with routine follow through and can be rather inconsiderate in social situations.

Orange

People in the orange team are noticeable by their energy, skill and creativity. The flexibility to use one's talents and abilities is important to Oranges. The orange personality feels stifled and performs poorly if there is excessive structure or if their employer is overly autocratic. People-oriented orange personalities thrive in environments that foster cooperation, competition, and friendship. However, because they are action-oriented, they lose patience with lengthy discussions and minutely detailed administrative work.

Consequently, a team's colors can be used by a leader to bring the team members together into a cohesive, well-coordinated picture that is geared for success. The leader is well on the way to producing amazing outcomes by enabling each team member to work in their areas of natural strength and inspiring them by speaking in a way that encourages harmony and teamwork.

CHAPTER 6

Three Things Leaders Don't Do

Over time, what we expect from leaders has evolved. The following were once connected to leadership but are no longer universally accepted as desirable traits for leadership today:

Below, we'll take a look at each of these features.

1. Management Vs. Leadership

Management and leadership are two different concepts. They are distinct yet complimentary processes. And while leaders set the course for the work to be done, they also need to use management abilities to lead their teams in a smooth and effective manner to the correct destination.

Management has been referred to as the:

the effective and efficient planning, organizing, staffing, directing, and control of organizational resources to achieve organizational goals.

Today, we would also include the duties of developing people and upholding a duty of care.

People in management positions are increasingly expected to demonstrate behaviors that might be more appropriately referred to as leadership behaviors, such as developing a compelling vision, inspiring and motivating their team, acting strategically, and facilitating change.

Without displaying leadership qualities, managers can still be highly competent, effective at their jobs, and valuable to their organizations.

However, one particular risk in these circumstances is that those being managed by such a person or group may mistakenly believe they are being led. There might be absolutely no leadership present, with no one establishing a vision and inspiring anyone. Over time, this could lead to significant issues.

Therefore, management and leadership are not mutually exclusive activities; rather, they are much more likely to be chosen and used as needed, depending on the situation.

2. Personality or Trait Theory

One of the earliest attempts to explain why successful leaders have certain traits is the trait theory. Significantly, rather than emphasizing leadership development, trait theories frequently emphasize the value of choosing the right leaders.

Long associated with leadership, charisma and confidence are seen as necessary for a leader to succeed. Despite how appealing this theory may seem, a leader who possesses these qualities may end up alienating their followers because they may mistakenly think they are more skilled than they actually are.

With today's rapid technological change, flatter organizational structures, and empowered employees, the command-and-control leadership techniques of the previous century are less suitable.

Similar to this, taking calculated risks and being assertive when making decisions can pay off handsomely. However, when they are not counterbalanced by a team's collective expertise, they can result in resentment, mistrust, fear, and even business failure.

Today's organizations place a high value on sharing knowledge, being creative, and taking the initiative to foresee and address the needs of stakeholders.

As a result, the "leader as hero" paradigm has largely been replaced by a more people-centered leadership style in which leaders demonstrate a willingness to act in the interests of their team, clients, and other stakeholders.

Therefore, it will be challenging for a leader to come across as authentic and credible unless their personal beliefs align with the organization's leadership brand.

3. Hierarchy

Although hierarchical ideas about leadership were once prevalent, this may no longer be the case. The role of leadership is evolving to include distributed activity. The field of education is where distributed leadership first emerged, and... Holacracy is another more recent nonhierarchical leadership model. In an organization that employs this model, departments are grouped into circles and sub-circles according to their roles and objectives. Sub-circles regularly meet and decide on their own while taking into account the requirements of the organization (the biggest, most inclusive circle). Sub-circles are represented by designated members who serve as intermediaries and ensure that the tasks assigned to them are completed. Everyone in this model has authority and responsibility, and they all use leadership abilities to manage themselves.

Leadership and Team Management

Here we will look at the actions that successful leaders must take in order to create and establish a management team network to successfully support the organization's strategies.

This will also provide guidance for managers who are involved in leading the strategic direction of their organizations.

Choosing an effective organizational structure requires taking into account the strategic direction and objectives of the organization, as well as the desired organizational culture, important activity areas for the organization, and the vital activity areas themselves. This is a crucial first action. The leaders must choose an organizational structure that will support the strategic direction being taken and an organizational culture that they will be attempting to build before any adjustments or new paths can be adopted. The network of management teams that is subsequently established will work with the structure and aid in creating the ideal culture.

Choosing a management team structure entails planning a network of management teams to meet the needs identified in the previous activity, as well as deciding on each team's structure, goals, roles, and responsibilities, as well as its size, location, and resource requirements. Each management team's member and team leader profiles are also identified. The planning done here will serve as the model for the new building when it is put into place. The ideal way to approach this planning is as a factual, needs-based activity. Size, location, team leader, and member profiles should all be determined by the team's job and goals. After the structure has been decided, any resource-related considerations should be addressed. Only after the teams have been assembled should existing and potential employees be evaluated against these.

Option 1: Evaluating Current Teams by identifying current management teams, analyzing current teams' objectives, evaluating current teams' performance, evaluating individual team leaders' performance, and comparing each management team profile with the newly defining requirements. This will be required in many, if not most, organizations because of ethical or legal limits. The results of this activity will just identify what are likely to be significant gaps and changes that will need to be made in order to fit the new criteria, as the existing teams are unlikely to be acceptable, other than in part.

Option 2: Dissolving Current Teams entails entirely dismantling the previous organization. This is the most radical approach, this one involves a complete reengineering. This is the best choice if it is possible, because the organization can go forward unimpeded by management teams that are partially or completely unfit for the new strategic direction.

Establishing the teams in their locations, choosing team leaders and team members, training each team in its new role, responsibilities, objectives, and operational activities, providing appropriate resources for each team, and putting the new network into operation are all steps in the implementation of the new management teams network. In the majority of organizations, this means doing so at all levels and both internally and externally. This step, which is crucial, needs to be managed as a significant project and as a major change effort. To oversee the modifications, a manager at the executive level ought to be chosen. Careful management of communication with all stakeholders, who will be many, active at various levels and both within and external to the organization, is required.

Implementing a Management Team Performance System entails developing a comprehensive system for evaluating team performance, keeping track of each team's performance, and taking the proper remedial action as needed. Effective employee appraisal systems are used by many organizations, although they typically only apply to operational staff and junior management. As the manager's activities typically have a higher negative or good influence, middle and senior managers must also be evaluated on a regular basis, ideally more frequently than operational personnel. Because of the level of influence and significance of the team's decisions and activities, this line of reasoning must also be applied to management teams.

The organization's leaders must always be aware of the performance levels of their management teams and take appropriate action to uphold or improve that performance level as needed. It is crucial to implement a continuous improvement and performance evaluation approach across the network of management teams. In the early phases of the teams' existence, the emphasis will be on raising awareness of and understanding for the goals of the team, as well as identifying the need for training and development to support any added or modified roles. The monitoring will prioritize maintaining consistency of performance as the team develops and matures, followed by enabling ongoing performance improvement. Performance evaluation must be a consistent and obvious process across the whole life cycle of each team.

Review and refresh the management team's network by scheduling routine evaluations of its appropriateness, evaluating each component's suitability in light of updated strategic objectives, comparing the network's structure to the current organizational structure, and making necessary adjustments to both its individual components and overall structure. Every year, a significant review should be conducted as a crucial component of reviewing and revising strategies and goals as part of the yearly strategic planning process. Minor or significant adjustments should be made at this review point to the network to ensure that it continues to meet the demands imposed by the updated strategic and operational objectives. Additionally, the state of the management team network should be discussed at least quarterly at the executive level so that any necessary corrective action can be decided.

In conclusion, creating a management team structure that works well is a crucial first step in making sure the organization's strategies are successfully implemented. The strategic and operational goals will not be accomplished without a strong network of management teams that is suited to the size and complexity of the organization and its strategic objectives. The achievement of objectives is fuelled by efficient management teams. If this network is poor or has flaws, it cannot succeed. It is the responsibility of the organization's executives to make sure that the management team network is powerful, active, and focused on achieving its goals both individually and as a whole.

CHAPTER 7

How to Become a Better Leader in The Workplace

At both the academic and organizational levels, attitudes toward leadership have shifted dramatically. Top-down autocratic leadership is now widely acknowledged to have much less relevance for modern organizations, which must contend with rapid change and struggle to survive in an intensely competitive and increasingly global marketplace.

There are therefore six types of power that leaders can employ, covering both traditional and contemporary conceptions of leadership. Among these, having knowledgeable leaders is especially beneficial. These leaders are respected and trusted because they are experts in their field. They are credible, and they have a claim to respect and obedience. Because of this, it is much simpler for these leaders to inspire and motivate their teams.

To be regarded favorably by their followers and other stakeholders, good leaders must be adaptable, flexible, ethical, and culturally sensitive. To maximize their performance, that of their team members, and that of the organization as a whole, today's and tomorrow's effective leaders will collaborate, consult, and distribute their power.

Knowing that their position can make them intimidating to the people they lead can help leaders take preventative measures. For instance, corporate executives decide how much people are paid and how secure their jobs are. Therefore, a good leader should make an effort to establish trust, be approachable, and communicate to others that it's acceptable to make mistakes and grow from them.

Effective leaders typically have the following characteristics: they are at ease with their roots, are self-aware, and are able to adapt as they move up the ranks without losing their authenticity. They can also articulate the connection between where they've been and where they're going.

Genuine leaders exhibit integrity, accountability, and bravery. Instead of trying to shape themselves into the type of leader they believe they should be, they remain true to who they are. They practice self-discipline, cultivate enduring relationships with others, and lead with meaning, purpose, and values. Authentic leaders create authentic organizations that are better equipped to provide long-term value for their clients and investors and less prone to mismanagement and corruption.

Last but not least, humility is thought to be a kind of quiet confidence where the person keeps an open mind to suggestions.

Rules for Effective Leadership

How you come across to your team members and employees makes all the difference between being a boss and being a leader. Bosses rely on their position of power to get people to do what they want, but effective leaders utilize their influence to inspire their teams. Instead of using fear and punishment to coerce conformity, effective leadership encourages people to look up to you and reach their greatest potential.

1. Seek To Motivate Others

You bring out the best in others when you inspire them. Team members who work for authoritarian management are afraid of receiving severe punishment for even the smallest infractions. On the surface, this may appear to be the best kind of leadership, but it simply results in high employee turnover and conflict.

By motivating others, you enable them to take initiative and accomplish more. Because you are having a good influence on everyone's thinking, it demonstrates strong leadership when everyone is working toward a goal and reaching the success they want to achieve.

Being passionate about the company's mission and implementing the company's values are two methods to inspire others. Being trustworthy and honest is also important since you need the trust of your team members in order to motivate and encourage them. Because your leadership style reflects who you are personally, it's critical to lead with a strong moral compass and base your judgments on it.

2. Show High Emotional Intelligence

Good leaders are aware of their own emotions as well as those of their team members. Your emotional intelligence abilities are demonstrated by the way you work with and support your team.

Because of this, effective leaders strive to inspire, direct, and advise their team rather than giving commands and being overbearing or demanding.

They are considerate and aware of how their team members are feeling. For instance, effective leaders are aware that everyone experiences bad days and that everyone learns differently. Some people learn best visually, while others learn best through doing. As a good leader, you must take into account each of these aspects when managing your team.

Leaders with strong emotional intelligence are able to respond to situations rather than just reacting to them. Anger, worry, or frustration can cloud your judgment and lead you to make poor choices. In the same way that you cannot force people to respect you, good leaders are aware that you cannot control everything. Respect must be earned.

Some people I've worked with in the past adhere to the 24-hour rule, which states that they shouldn't reply to or make a significant choice before they've had some time to consider it and analyze it. Although it may not always be possible, it's crucial to take your time and carefully consider your options before acting. You must decide based on clarity, not on haste or fright. It is a sign of great emotional intelligence to greet your staff, strike up a discussion, and make others feel valued. This creates a sense of community where communication may occur without worry for condemnation. *"Leadership is an action, not a position." – Donald McGannon*

3. Demonstrate Hard Work

Working hard shows commitment, which inspires others to follow suit. Leaders work hard when they are on time, fulfill deadlines, and see initiatives through to completion.

Hard effort from a leadership perspective doesn't mean that you should solely focus on yourself and ignore other people. By assisting team members with their requirements and taking the initiative on all tasks, effective leaders show that they are willing to work hard.

Team members are inspired to finish their task because they want to be productive when they see you being helpful, following through, and showing intuition.

Working hard demonstrates that you, as a leader, are not above any of the duties at work but rather that you care enough to lighten the load for co-workers.

Instead of giving orders from the side lines and making everyone do the work you don't want to do, good leaders work hard because it motivates their team.

4. Pay Attention To Your Workers

A healthy workplace requires effective communication to encourage employee innovation and boost morale.

In today's world, a leader who doesn't have all the answers is seen as weak, but this is untrue. Nobody has all the knowledge, and that is completely acceptable.

A competent leader sets aside their ego and builds strong relationships with their team members so that each and every one of their opinions is respected and utilized to strengthen the business as a whole. This is why it's so important to operate as a team, even as a leader, because you never know who can come up with a last-minute solution or offer experience-based guidance.

Considering that everyone has had different experiences, good leaders are patient and approach challenges with empathy.

Although it is required to obey a boss, most people choose to do so because they feel led by them.

People look up to good leaders because they boost their subordinates up rather than looking down on them. Building trusting relationships and being a relatable person need doing this.

5. Good Leaders Avoid Micromanagement

Most essential, effective leaders support their team members' independence and freedom of expression. They avoid micromanagement because they are aware of how it prevents employees from developing personally and creatively.

Micromanaging is all about having total control and results from insecurity. Employees are starved of their creative talents by micromanagement, which results in dissatisfaction, resentment, and a high rate of turnover.

This indicates that they do not oversee or supervise every small aspect of their workers' work or how they complete their tasks. People have the right to choose the method that works best for them, just as there are various learning styles. It's possible that what works for you won't for someone else.

Because it makes employees dependent and makes them afraid to make decisions on their own, therefore micromanagement is dangerous and counterproductive.

However, effective leaders create teams with individuals they can trust and let employees play to their strengths. When you put your employees' trust, you're encouraging the development of their creative skills and abilities.

You never know how far you can go with the right team. Therefore, compassion and trust are essential for increasing team output.

CHAPTER 8

The Power of Servant Leadership

Typically, the concepts of servant and leader are viewed as being in opposition to one another. A paradox occurs when two opposites are combined in a unique and meaningful way. Servant leadership's fundamental tenet is both logical and obvious. Since the Industrial Revolution, managers have a tendency to see people as objects, and organizations see employees as cogs in a machine. We have seen a change in that long-held belief over the last few decades.

This has created a need for a better leadership style, one that prioritizes serving others above all else, including employees, clients, and the community. Servant leadership places a strong emphasis on giving more to others, approaching work holistically, encouraging a sense of community, and delegating decision-making authority.

What exactly is Servant Leadership?

Servant leadership is a leadership philosophy in which the leader is first and foremost a servant. Servant leaders put the needs of their group and the organization ahead of their own objectives. It is a form of selfless leadership in which a leader has a strong inclination to work for the benefit of others.

The servant leader is someone who puts others before themselves. The distinction can be seen in the attention paid by the servant leader, who puts other people's needs above all else.

In essence, servant-leadership is a way of being that has the potential to bring about positive change in all facets of our society. It is a long-term, transformative approach to life and work.

Someone who gracefully navigates a dispute using diplomacy as a guide is exhibiting servant leadership.

Finding a compromise on policy while maintaining one's morals and values is the hallmark of servant leadership. Being self-aware is the foundation of servant leadership. It involves being aware of both your individual and the collective SWOT analysis of your team.

The leader is not always in the right when there is servant leadership at play. In fact, even if it means deviating from their intended course, an effective servant leader must look for the best way to move forward. A servant leader is courageous but kind in their forgiveness and compromise. A servant leader makes decisions while keeping an open mind, exercising discernment, and taking into account sincerity and thoughtful opinions.

A servant leader is service oriented rather than subservient. A distinction exists. One acts out of fear, while the other does so with courage in both mission and approach. A servant leader prioritizes the needs of others over their own. Finally, a servant leader overcomes the desire to be right in favor of acting morally.

On the surface, servant leadership may seem powerless and weak. It's actually the complete opposite, though. It takes a great deal of character strength to be a source of empowerment that inspires others to take on leadership roles. An identity that is independent of approval and status, as well as a healthy sense of self-worth, are necessary. One needs emotional stability that has been developed through extensive self-reflection and knowledge. Above all, it is necessary to be transparent in one's speech, deeds, and life. In other words, servant leadership calls for personal integrity. Because people are quick to spot lies.

Given how powerful servant leadership is, conflicts are sometimes inevitable. It breaks with convention. It provides inspiration. The gap between "governors" and "the governed" can be narrowed through servant leadership. It helps others reach their full potential. As opposed to hierarchy, servant leadership is team-oriented. The best-paid or person with the most prestigious title may not always be the servant leader. In highly competitive environments, servant leaders forge relationships based on cooperation and trust. The goal of servant leadership is to look beyond the short-term pleasure and immediate gratification to the medium- to long-term realm of justice and rightness.

Relationship Qualities and Abilities For Good Servant Leadership

The capacity to collaborate and relate to people is a crucial component of effective leadership. Successful leadership in the area of interacting to and communicating with others is characterized by a specific set of traits. The eleven characteristics are listed below.

1. Availability

An effective leader is accessible and in touch with the public. The capacity to identify needs and be able to act on them instantly and flexibly is a crucial leadership trait.

2. Approachability

A good leader welcomes inquiries and maintains an open door policy. A culture of justice rather than judgment is fostered through good leadership, which fosters transparency and honesty.

3. Promoting Peaceful Relationships

A good leader is proactive in fostering harmony because they understand how important harmonious relationships are. Instead of fighting, harmonious outcomes are what lead to success. Maintaining the least amount of dispute and discord is a priority for good leadership.

4. Proper Usage Of Power

The hallmark of effective leadership is sensitivity to the appropriate use of their authority and, conversely, to its abuse. A competent leader won't abuse their position of power to advance their own interests or to exert dictatorial control over others. Successful leaders are wise and sensitive to the appropriateness of the situation when using their positional power.

5. Self-Motivated

To inspire themselves and others, effective leaders develop and use goals. They are aware of the significance of both professional and personal development. Successful leaders take the necessary steps to stay current in their area and to improve their knowledge and skills. Successful leaders inspire others around them in addition to inspiring personal growth in themselves.

6. Provide Support

Effective managers can offer emotional support to individuals they are in charge of. They value positive reinforcement and confidence-building, and they also express gratitude for a job well done.

7. Fostering Team Spirit and Motivation

A good leader challenges their team members to maintain high standards of performance by offering rewards and motivators.

8. Confidentiality

Conferencing and meetings organized by good leaders are conducted in a trusting environment. They conduct themselves with adequate discretion and regard for other people

9. Clear Communication

A good communicator makes for a good leader. Their leadership involves clearly outlining the goals and steps needed to complete a task. They make specific, doable, and quantifiable goals.

10. Group Dynamics Understanding

A good leader is familiar with the dynamics of group interactions. Successful leaders know how to manage conflict in their groups while minimizing discord. They are adept at fostering a sense of team cohesiveness and are inclusive. For the best outcomes, they are skilled at balancing the group's strengths and shortcomings.

Destructive Traits A Leader Should Avoid

Everyone desires to be led by an effective leader, but let's face it, some leaders are simply ineffective. Whether on the sports field, the battlefield, or the sales floor, terrible leaders share certain traits in common; they typically are...

1. Dismissive. Some leaders have a "my way or the highway" mentality, but their teams despise it, especially when they persist in doing something wrong or stupid. An ineffective leader won't pay attention to any of the team members.
2. Egotistical. Nobody wants to work for a haughty tyrant who considers himself or herself to be supreme. Leaders with large egos, often place the blame on others and accept credit when others succeed. They also have a propensity to be distant, which turns others off and promotes bad communication.

3. Lacking Empathy. They will unsubscribe from the cause and find another where their effort is appreciated if you don't care about your employees because that will make them feel irrelevant and unappreciated.

4. Grudge-bearing. A good leader forgets personal offense and moves on, especially if they want to create a functional environment. By contrast, a poor leader holds on to personal offense and lets it affect everyone else's work environment.

5. Pessimism. A good leader makes his team feel protected, but a bad leader encourages conflict, turmoil, and disagreement. To be honest, there have been many successful presidents who have used conflict to their advantage, but those leaders are typically violently overthrown in a coup. and if you're a leader, you generally don't want that.

6. Inconsistency. Some folks may go nuts over this particular subject. If the person in charge is constantly altering what they want, it is impossible to build a productive environment. They will never be satisfied, and it is a waste of time and resources for everyone to pursue unattainable goals.

7. Lack Of Transparency. Granted, a leader shouldn't always share every detail with their team (such as pay grades and salaries), but it's crucial to ensure everyone is on the same page when it comes to operational goals. Employees regularly come up against a wall of confusion due to a lack of clear guidance brought on by covert objectives.

8. Exhausted. An overworked boss is tense, irritable, and, probably most importantly, demonstrates to staff that work-life balance is unimportant, which is a negative outlook for people who frequently have obligations outside of work.

CHAPTER 9

Characteristics Of The Servant-Leader

After carefully examining the qualities of servant-leadership for a number of years, a set of traits of the servant-leader have been identified. Central to the growth of servant leaders are the qualities listed below:

By actively listening, a servant leader can ascertain the group's will and aid in its clarification. Gaining awareness of one's inner voice and attempting to decipher the messages being sent by one's body, spirit, and mind are also included in the definition of listening.

Empathy: It's important to accept and value each person for the unique qualities they possess as well as the contributions they make to the workplace. The most effective servant-leaders are those who have honed their ability to listen empathically.

Healing: The ability to heal is a strong catalyst for change and integration. The ability to heal oneself and others at work is one of the greatest benefits of servant leadership.

Awareness: Knowledge helps one comprehend moral and ethical dilemmas. It makes it easier to take a more comprehensive, integrated approach to most situations.

Persuasion: A servant-leader tries to persuade others rather than force them to do something. One of the most obvious differences between the servant-leadership model and the conventional authoritarian model is provided by this particular component. The servant-leader is skilled at fostering group consensus.

Conceptualization: Short-term operational goals are the traditional manager's main concern. Servant leaders work to develop their capacity for dreaming big dreams.

One must think outside of the box in order to conceptualize a problem (or organization) from a perspective that is different from their everyday experience.

Foresight: With the help of foresight, a servant-leader is able to comprehend the lessons learned from the past, the realities of the present, and the likely effects of a decision on the future. It is also deeply rooted within the intuitive mind.

Stewardship: servant leadership is similar to stewardship in that both entail a dedication to meeting the needs of others. Additionally, it places a stronger emphasis on using openness and persuasion than control.

Commitment to employee growth: The servant-leader is aware of the enormous responsibility to use all of his or her resources to foster the personal, professional, and spiritual development of staff members.

Community-building: The servant-leader believes that much has been lost in recent human history as a result of the shift from small communities to big institutions as the primary influence on people's lives. This awareness prompts the servant-leader to look for ways to foster a sense of community among those who work for a particular institution.

Calling: Do your employees think you are willing to put aside your own interests in order to advance the company? The desire to help others comes naturally to servant leaders. This idea of having a calling to serve is deeply ingrained and based on values. When given the chance, servant leaders will seize the chance to improve the lives of their coworkers, the organization, and the community—never for their own gain—in order to serve others in the organization.

Nurturing The Spirit: A servant leader is someone who recognizes the universal desire of people to participate in personally fulfilling endeavors. Through sincere compliments and encouraging recognition, the servant-leader feeds the individual's spirit. No one is being harsh or personally attacked by criticisms. Through methods that honor the value of employees' dedication to worthwhile endeavors, the joy of the workplace is celebrated. The servant leader encourages employees to consider the significance of both the organization's challenges and successes and to draw lessons from both.

Chapter 10

The Advantages Of Servant Leadership

Stronger teams: Through their dedication to the group, servant leaders earn the respect of their subordinates, which fosters harmony, fosters increased teamwork, and fosters productive behavior.

Conducive workplace: In an organization, working alongside the leader fosters a positive workplace where interactions are more constructive and there is less competition to impress the leader through petty political squabbles.

Alignment of personal and professional goals: A servant leader's encouragement and support of professional and personal growth enable staff members to harmonize their own goals with those of the company.

The improved employee commitment, engagement, and loyalty to the company ultimately boosts output and profits.

Increased organizational agility: Teams that have their leaders' support are more adaptable to a changing environment, resulting in an agile organization.

Leaders' support for professional growth enhances the learning and development of employees, allowing for the augmentation of strengths and the addressing of weaknesses.

Leadership Training: Team members gain responsibility and ownership while working with their servant leaders, which strengthens their leadership skills.

Employee motivation is enhanced by servant leadership, which encourages employees to exercise greater creativity and innovation.

People-centered corporate culture: The philosophy fosters and develops a people-centered corporate culture.

Reduces employee churn: Motivated employees are more likely to stick around a company and continue contributing to the accomplishment of its goals.

Drawbacks of Servant Leadership

- Servant leaders may not possess an adequate understanding of service and the business as a whole.

- It's possible that servant leaders lack the desire to help others, making the theory useless.

- Servant leadership depends on its team's moral foundation.

- Leaders may find the servant leadership concept time-consuming and labor-intensive.

- The authenticity required for servant leadership is daunting and challenging to attain.

- Servant leaders run the risk of being seen as weak, which would reduce their formal authority.

- Lack of confidence - Employees are expected to make decisions and take responsibility for them, which may not be possible if a worker finds it challenging to see the big picture and lacks the confidence to make decisions that will advance the company.

- Slower decision making can result from consultative decision making.

How to Awaken The Leader In You - 10 Important Steps To Developing Your Leadership Skills

"The miracle power that elevates the few is to be found in their industry, application, and perseverance, under the promptings of a brave determined spirit." - Mark Twain

It's a popular belief among motivational experts that leaders are made, not born. I would make the complete opposite case. I really believe that despite being deprogrammed along the way, we are all born leaders. We were born leaders as youngsters, with a natural aptitude for inspiring others to support us in achieving our goals. We were humble and inquiring, constantly thirsty for education, and possessed creative imaginations. We also understood exactly what we wanted and were relentless and determined to attain it. Why then is it so challenging for grownups to achieve this? What actually occurred?

Growing up, we become accustomed to hearing the words "No," "Don't," and "Can't." No! Avoid doing this. Avoid doing that. This is impossible for you to accomplish. No, you can't. No! Many of our parents instructed us to be silent and refrain from annoying the grownups with pointless inquiries. As we progressed through high school, this pattern persisted, with teachers dictating what we could do and what we couldn't do. The main one, institutionalized formal education known as college or university, then impacted many of us. Unfortunately, the traditional educational system educates kids how to be courteous order takers for the corporate world rather than how to become leaders. Most people learn how to obey and deftly follow regulations in order to keep the corporate machine running, instead of learning to be creative, independent, self-reliant, and think for themselves.

The process of unlearning through self-remembering and self-honoring is therefore necessary if you want to develop the Leader within you to live your highest life. You'll need to have courage to open the door to your inner attic, where your childhood dreams are stored, and enter your heart if you want to be a successful leader once more. Here are ten simple steps you can take to reawaken the Leader in you and reignite your drive for greatness, based on my more than ten years of study in the fields of leadership and human development.

1. Modesty. Humility is the first step towards leadership. You must first humble yourself like a young child and be prepared to serve others if you want to be a very successful leader. Nobody likes to follow a haughty person. Keep your innocence, your curiosity, and your thirst for knowledge. What is greatness, after all, except knowledge added to knowledge added to knowledge? Excellence is constantly seeking improvement and growth. Being modest makes you truly curious about other people because you want to learn from them. Additionally, as listening is the most important leadership communication skill, you will be a much better listener since you want to learn and develop. People will naturally be interested in you and listen to what you have to say when they perceive that you are truly interested in them and listening to them.

2. Adhere to Your Happiness. No matter how busy you are, make time for what you enjoy doing. Others become more alive and energetic when they are. People around you are compelled by your presence while you are pursuing your passions. You will become a charismatic leader as a result. Set aside time each week, ideally two or three hours each day, to explore your interests, whether they are in writing, acting, painting, drawing, photography, sports, reading, dancing, networking, or starting your own business. I have faith that you'll find the time. You would be amazed at how much time is wasted if you were to videotape yourself for a day.

3. Think Big. You need a dream that is bigger than life if you want to be bigger than life. Small aspirations will not benefit you or anyone else. Dreaming large and tiny both require the same amount of time. Be Big and Bold, then! Your One Big Dream should be written down. The one that makes you most excited. Always remember to be big and unrealistic rather than little and practical! Go for the biggest honors in your field—the Gold, the Pulitzer, the Nobel, the Oscar. List every single reason why you CAN attain your ambition after you've put it down, rather than focusing on the reasons why you can't.

4. SWOT On Yourself. Strengths, Weaknesses, Opportunities, and Threats, also known as SWOT. Despite being a strategic management tool taught at Stanford and Harvard Business Schools and employed by significant multinational corporations, it may be applied just as successfully to your personal leadership development. It is possible to access self-knowledge, self-remembering, and self-honoring with this key. List all of your strengths, including your accomplishments, to start. Then list all of your shortcomings and what needs to be strengthened. Include any uncertainties, worries, fears, or anxieties you may have. The dragons and demons that are manning the entrance to your inner attic are these. You can start to kill them by bringing them to awareness. Next, make a list of all the opportunities you perceive for putting your abilities to use. Finally, list all of the threats or barriers that are keeping you from attaining your goals or that you anticipate facing on the journey

5. Vision. We lose our essence when we don't have a vision. It's improbable that you will be able to lead yourself or others to victory if you can't picture yourself receiving that trophy and feel the tears of joy running down your cheeks. Think about what it would be like to realize your dream. You can sense it with your eyes, nose, palate, ears, and gut.

6. Perseverance. Victory belongs to those who pursue it most fervently and persistently. Make sure to act consistently each day now that you have a dream. I advise carrying out at least 5 daily actions that will help you get closer to your goal.

7. Find a Mentor. Choose a mentor for yourself. Preferably someone who has had significant success in your sector already. Never hesitate to ask. Nothing stands to lose. Finding local mentoring programmes is made easy with the help of Google. Spend some time reading the autobiographies of influential figures you like in addition to finding mentors. Learn as much as you can from their experiences, and take some of their effective coping mechanisms to heart.

8. Be Authentic. Never replicate or imitate them like a parrot; instead, use your relationships with mentors and your research on outstanding leaders as models or points of reference. Everyone has a completely distinct approach to leadership. Every type of leader may be found in history books, from the outspoken, extroverted, and loud to the soft-spoken, introverted, and quiet, and everything in between. Gandhi, who was unassuming and modest, or Jimmy Carter, a soft-spoken peanut farmer who went on to become president of the United States and win the Nobel Peace Prize, were as effective as loud and showy Churchill or Margaret Thatcher's strong leadership style. I admire Les Brown as a motivational speaker. But if I copy Les Brown, I'd be a second or third rate Les Brown, at best, instead of a first-rate John Maximillian. Be yourself, your best self, always competing against yourself and bettering yourself, and you will become a first rate YOU instead of a second rate somebody else.

9. Keep Your Word. You lose power each time you break your word. Successful leaders are dependable and reliable. Even if you can have all the material possessions and wealth in the world, you only have one reputation in life. Your word holds value. Respect it.

10. Give Generously. Givers are leaders. A universal law that is as reliable as gravity is activated when you give: Life gives to the giver and takes from the taker. Giving more results in receiving more. Give love, respect, support, and compassion if you want to receive more of the same in return. Be a role model for others. Give back to your neighborhood. As a leader, you can only achieve your goals by first assisting a sufficient number of others in achieving theirs.

We make a livelihood by what we get, but we create a life by what we give, as Sir Winston Churchill famously stated.

CHAPTER 11

Conclusion

Workplace leadership is a complex blend of both hard and soft skills with a strong emphasis on interpersonal relationships and communication.

Many facets of effective leadership can be learned with practice, even though not everyone will naturally possess the necessary traits. You'll be well on your way to becoming a better leader if you work on self-awareness, recognize your strengths and weaknesses, and use the appropriate leadership approach for the circumstances at hand.

Getting other people to follow you is the essence of leadership. Anyone who can persuade others to follow them, has the makings of a leader.

Leadership occurs at all levels of organizations and society, not just among those who hold formally designated "leadership positions."

Although it is always a multifaceted role, leadership can mean different things to different people, different cultures, and in different situations.

The success of followers is made possible by effective leadership. It establishes a course, creates a vision, and makes adjustments as necessary. Consequently, planning your course to "win" as a group or an organization is the essence of leadership. It's exciting, dynamic, and motivating.

www.ingramcontent.com/pod-product-compliance
Lightning Source LLC
Chambersburg PA
CBHW071128240526
45465CB00024B/1545